BLUES TRACKS

The **ultimate backing track** collection for guitar

ROBERT BROWN
WAYNE RIKER
MARK DZIUBA

Alfred, the leader in educational music publishing, and the National Guitar Workshop, one of America's finest guitar schools, have joined forces to bring you the best, most progressive educational tools possible. We hope you will enjoy this book and encourage you to look for other fine products from Alfred and the National Guitar Workshop.

This book was acquired, edited, and produced by Workshop Arts, Inc., the publishing arm of the National Guitar Workshop.
Nathaniel Gunod, acquisitions, managing editor
Burgess Speed, senior editor
Timothy Phelps, interior design
Ante Gelo, music typesetter
CD recorded at Standing Room Only Recording Studio, Fontana, CA; Workshop Sounds, High Falls, New York; and Soundwave, Inc., Washington, D.C.
Engineered by Robert Brown, Mark Dziuba, and Darrell Ashley
Music composed by Robert Brown, Mark Dziuba, and Wayne Riker
Guitars: Wayne Riker, Robert Brown, and Mark Dziuba
Keyboards: Robert Lanuza, Robert Brown, and Mark Dziuba
Bass: Fred Ubaldo, Jr., Robert Brown, and Mark Dziuba
Drums: Tom Versen
Saxophone: Bob Campbell

Cover photographs: Lead Guitar: © Gibson / Courtesy of Gibson USA • Bass Guitar: © Schecter / Courtesy of Schecter • Drums: © Drum Workshop / Courtesy of Drum Workshop • Keyboard: © Yamaha / Courtesy of Yamaha Music • Background © dreamstime.com / Beholdereye

Alfred Music Publishing Co., Inc.
P.O. Box 10003
Van Nuys, CA 91410-0003
alfred.com

ISBN-10: 0-7390-8602-2 (Book & CD)
ISBN-13: 978-0-7390-8602-5 (Book & CD)

2

Contents

Introduction

Many consider practicing a necessary evil, a chore; or BORING! Endless scales and arpeggios are important but, unfortunately, they sometimes get tedious. Perhaps the most enjoyable way to practice techniques is by incorporating them into your solos while you jam. Blues Tracks is the ideal tool to provide accompaniments and techniques that will improve your playing while you solo.

There are over 30 tunes included that range from simple to complex, all in the style of the seminal artists from the history of blues, including Big Bill Broonzy, Eric Clapton, Robert Cray, B.B. King, and many others. You won't just be practicing techniques; you will actually be crafting your own authentic blues guitar sound.

This book provides lead sheets, tips, scales, and original accompaniment tracks that are long enough to let you stretch out and experiment as your chops develop. Scales are recommended for every tune and are shown in standard music notation, TAB, and guitar neck diagrams. Rhythmic notation and licks are even provided for select tunes. In the back of the book, there is also a collection of licks and melodies for you to add to your vocabulary.

Blues Tracks is the perfect way for you to make the most out of your practice time and seriously advance your improvisational skills. Stop being bored and enjoy practicing by starting right now!

About the Authors

Robert Brown, a guitarist and composer, was on the faculty of the National Guitar Workshop from 1984 to 1991. During those years, he taught everything from blues to jazz, songwriting, and MIDI seminars. He is the author of many other books published by the National Guitar Workshop and Alfred Music Publishing. Robert Brown is currently living and working in Nashville, TN.

Wayne Riker has been a guitar teacher and performer for over twenty five years, playing and teaching all styles of music. After earning a degree in english and music from Farleigh Dickinson University in 1973, he went on to graduate from the Guitar Institute of Technology in 1980. He has been an instructor at the National Guitar Workshop's California campus since its inception in 1990. Wayne is a teacher and freelance guitarist in the San Diego area and conducts workshops around the United States.

Mark Dziuba, a guitarist, bassist, and composer, received his master of music degree in theory and composition from the University of Illinois in 1987. While there, he attended workshops and lectures with composers such as John Cage, Milton Babbitt, and Vladimir Ussachevsky. He currently serves on the music faculty of the State University of New York at New Paltz. Mark is a senior faculty member of the National Guitar Summer Workshop where he has worked with John Scofield, Ronnie Earl, Tal Farlow, Mark Egan, and Larry Carlton. He also runs the Workshop's recording studio, Workshop Sounds. He is the author of *The Big Book of Jazz Guitar Improvisation*, also published by the National Guitar Workshop and Alfred Music Publishing. The Mark Dziuba Quartet performs regularly in the New York area.

How to Use This Book and MP3 CD

This book and CD allows you to be the lead guitarist in a band. You'll play solos with a great rhythm section backing you up.

For each tune on the CD, you will be given the following information:

1. The key

2. How many choruses there are

3. When other soloists will play

4. The chord progression

In the book, each chord progression is followed by scale diagrams. Use them as a guide to help you improvise.

1. The tonic of each scale is displayed as a white dot.

2. Most scales and modes are shown using one position.

3. When scales are displayed using the whole fretboard, at first, break the scale into four-or five-fret sections, this will make it much easier to manage the scale.

Here are some suggestions that will make your practice time more effective:

- Spend some time just listening to each track.

- Pay attention to the form each piece takes (repeats, coda, etc.).

- Learn the notes as well as the shape of each scale on the fingerboard.

- Sing your solos before you play them (great for ear training).

Tuning

 Track 1 Make sure your guitar is in tune with this MP3 CD by tuning to this track.

Track 2

J. B. Goode's Blues

Let's get started with a standard blues in A.

Fast blues in A

A Minor Pentatonic

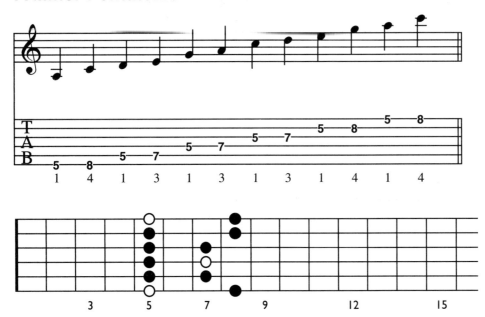

A Major Pentatonic

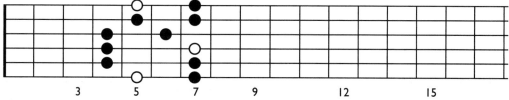

A Blues Scale

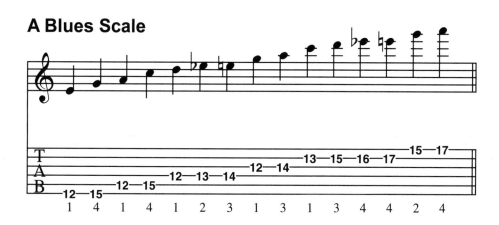

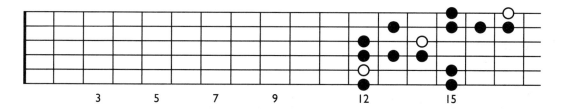

Form
21 choruses. Intro chorus, then play rhythm part on choruses 11, 13, 15, and 21. Chorus 21 is the intro chorus again. Standard ending.

Track 3

Hide and Seek

This tune is a classic shuffle blues pattern which can be heard in many songs, particularly Jimmy Reed songs like "Bright Lights, Big City" and "You Got Me Runnin'...You Got Me Hidin'." Play the major pentatonic over the I chord (A7). Refer to Appendix B for specific lick ideas over the IV chord (D7) and the V chord (E7).

Play 10 times

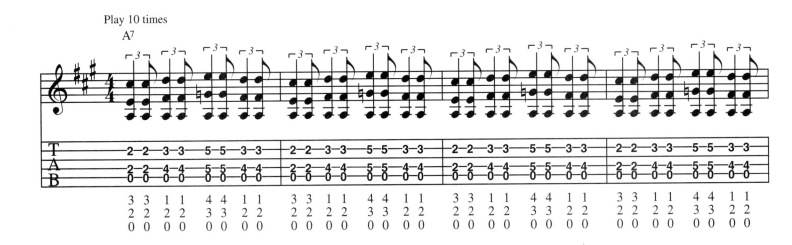

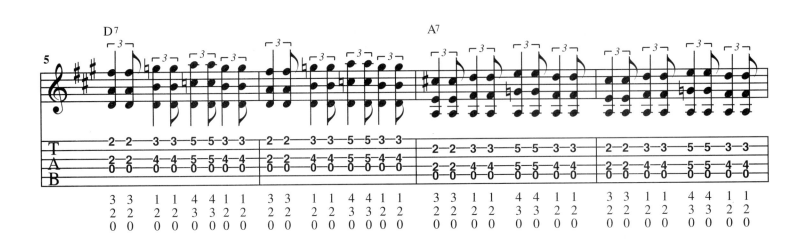

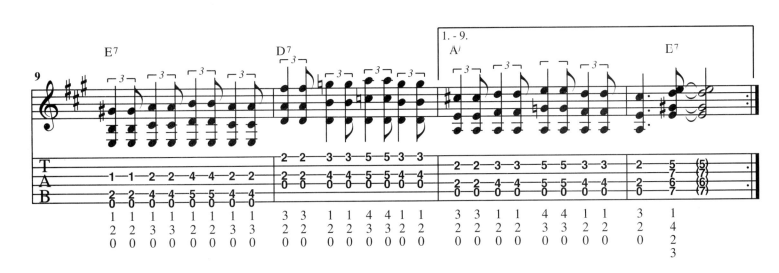

A Minor Pentatonic

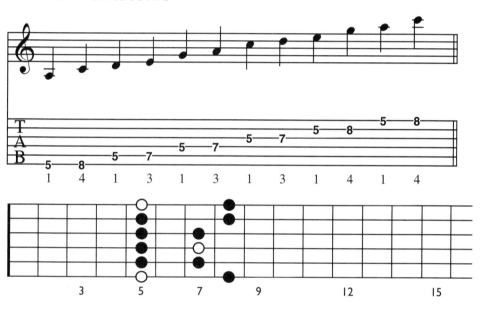

A Major Pentatonic

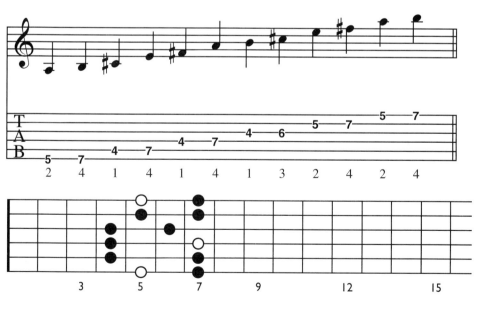

Form
Play rhythm part on choruses 1, 5, 8, and 10. Solo on all other choruses.

Track 4

Six Floors Under

This tune is based on the rhythmic pattern from the rhythm & blues tune, "Killing Floor." Experiment with both blues scales. Use the A Blues scale to help make a stronger statement. Appendix B contains some more lick ideas to use over the IV (D7) and V (E7) chords. Listen to the bluesman Earl King to get a feel for this style.

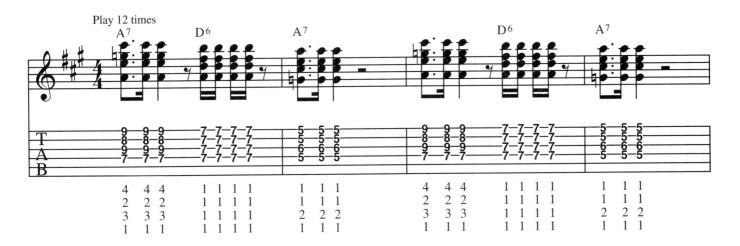

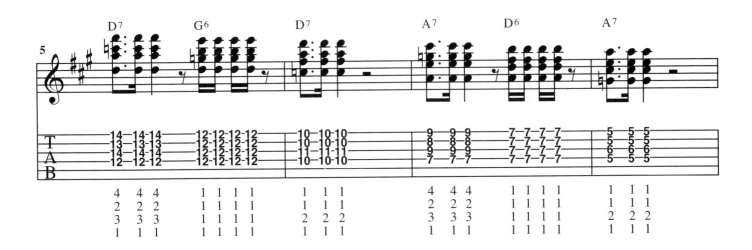

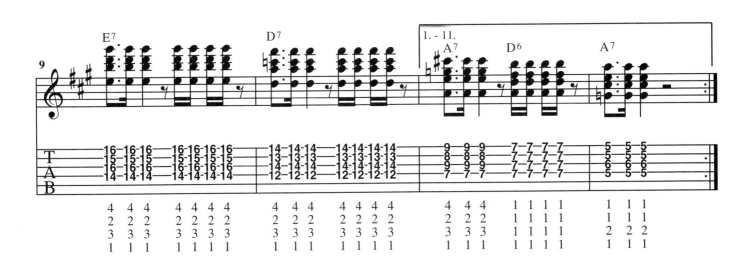

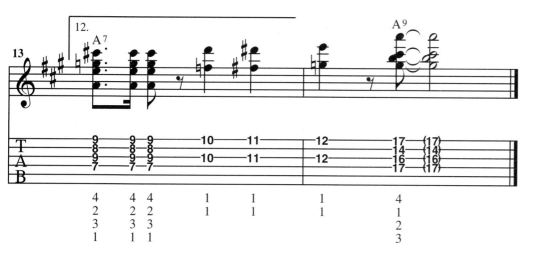

A Blues

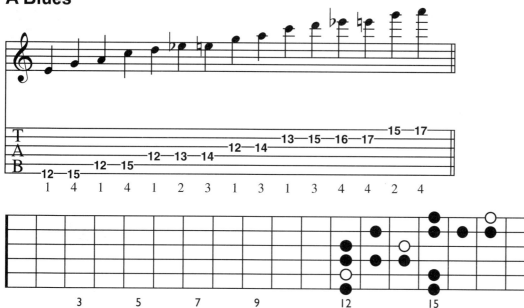

F# Blues

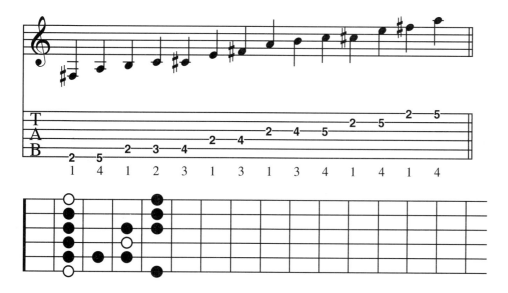

Form
Play rhythm on choruses 1, 6, 7, and 12. Solo on all other choruses.

St. James Blues

Even though this is in A Minor, you are still going to use scales that you use in an A Major blues.

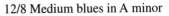

12/8 Medium blues in A minor

A Minor Pentatonic

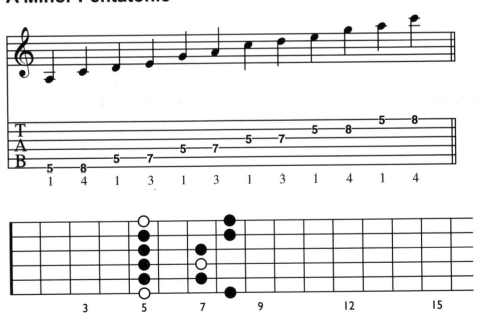

A Blues Scale

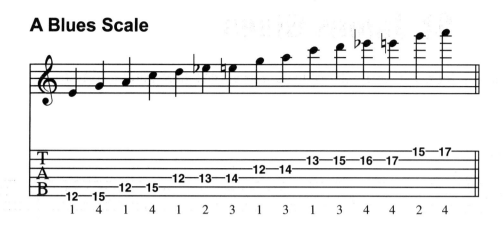

1   4   1   4   1   2   3   1   3   1   3   4   4   2   4

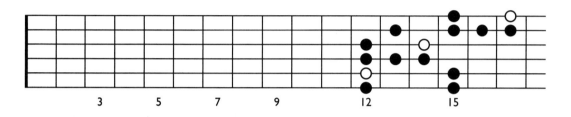

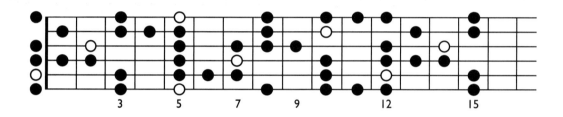

Form
10 choruses. Play rhythm on choruses 4 and 8. Long ending on last chorus.

B. B.'s Minor Blues

This is a standard minor blues inspired by the iconic playing of B.B. King.

Slow blues in A minor

A Minor Pentatonic

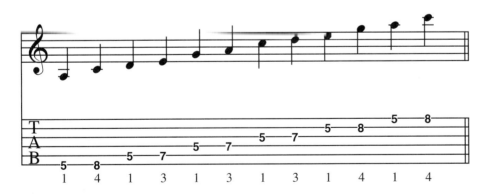

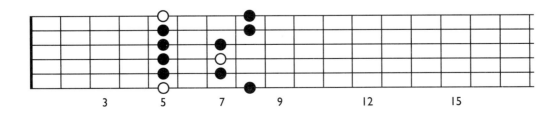

A Blues Scale

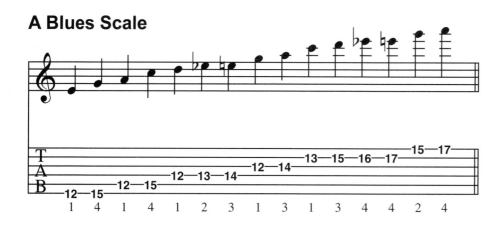

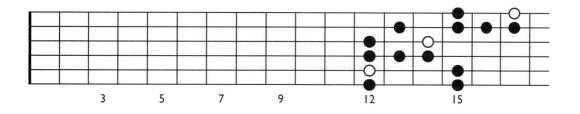

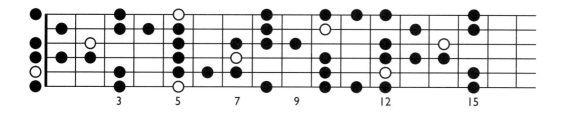

Form

8 choruses. Starts with the E+7 chord while you solo. Play rhythm on chorus 6 and solo over all others. Chorus 5 is in stop time.

A. M. Blues

This is a typical rock minor blues. Pay careful attention to the Bmin7♭5 going to the E7♯9. This is an excellent opportunity to use an interesting sound from the melodic minor scale: Super Locrian (the 7th mode of the melodic minor, also known as the altered dominant scale). Try to hear the difference between the chord scales, and concentrate on the common tones (notes shared by two or more chords). This kind of focus will help you hear much more. Remember to learn the notes and not just the patterns of this new scale.

Play 10 times and fade

E Super Locrian

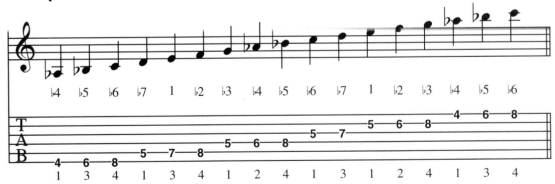

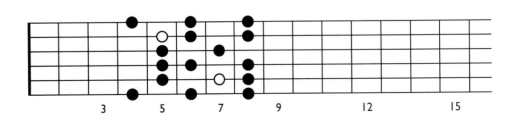

A Minor Pentatonic

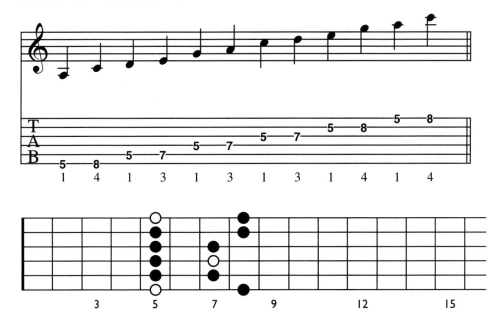

D Dorian

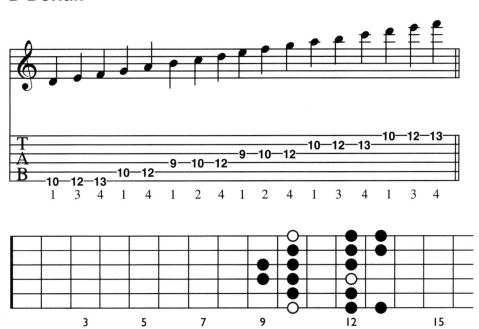

Form
Repeat entire song ten times and fade. 2nd guitar solos the fourth time through.

Track 8

Every Day with the Blues

This tune uses a classic rhythm & blues riff which has been played in many blues standards, particularly those on any of B.B. King's recordings with full horn sections. Switch back and forth liberally between the B♭ and G Blues scales. Check out Appendix B on page 77 for licks to use over the E♭7 and F7.

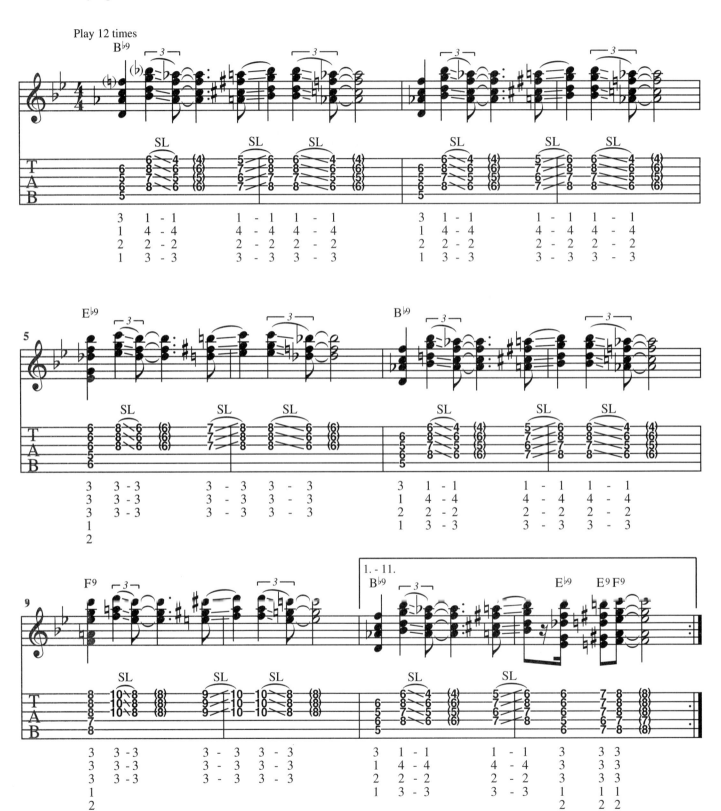

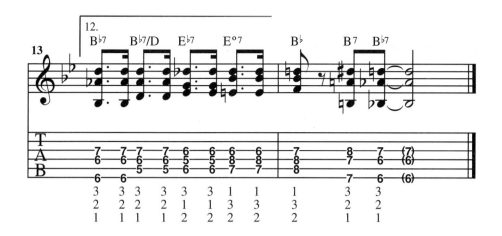

B♭ Blues

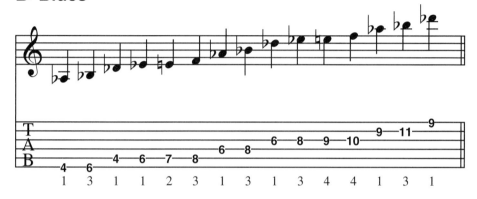

G Blues

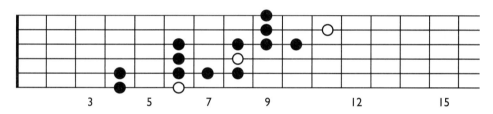

Form
Play rhythm on choruses 1, 6, 7, and 12. Solo on all other choruses.

Jazz Blues

This is a typical jazz-style blues with a shuffle feel. The ii–V–I progression is used to add more harmonic motion to this blues style. Being able to play over this kind of progression is very important as it is used and heard everywhere. Try to think in the key of the ii–V and play from within that key. For example, in measure four we are in the key of B♭: Cm7 is the ii and F7 is the V. This will obviously require a lot of work to use effectively. Page 21 has some examples of how to play over a ii–V progression. Try writing your own ii–V licks!

ii–V Lick (measures 4–5)

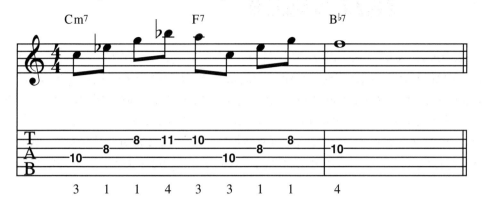

ii–V Idea (measures 7–9)

Form
Repeat the entire form five times.

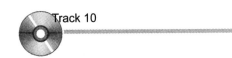

K. C.'s Blues

This is a standard blues in C.

C

C Minor Pentatonic

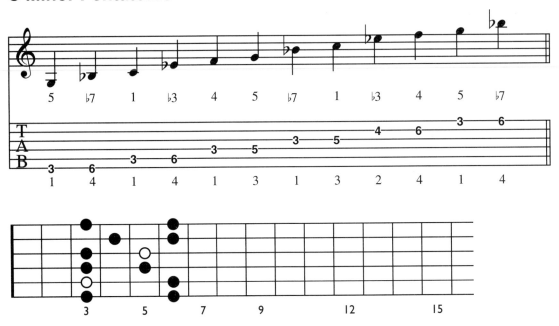

C Major Pentatonic

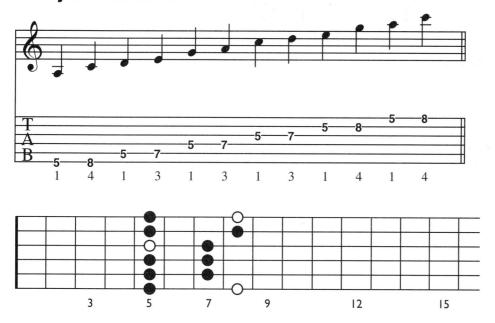

C Blues Scale

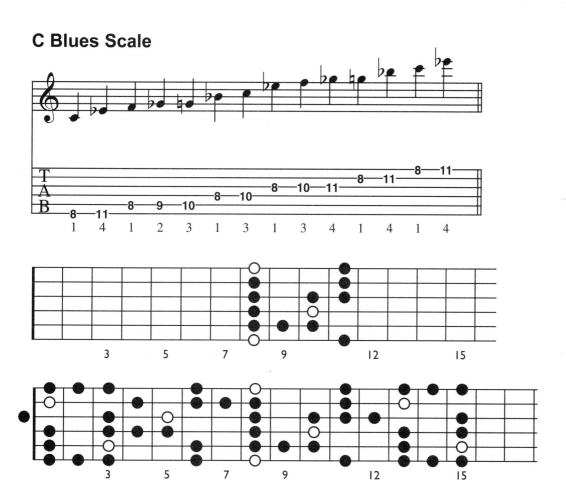

Form

13 choruses. Intro chorus, then play rhythm part on choruses 4, 7, and 10.
Long ending on last chorus. Stop time is used in choruses 3 and 11.

J. C.'s Blues

Here is another common C blues.

C

Fast pattern blues in C

C Minor Pentatonic

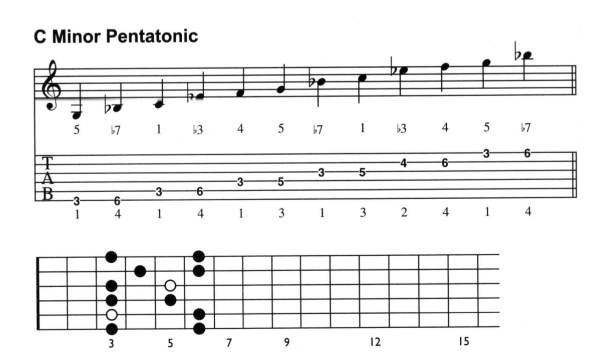

C Major Pentatonic

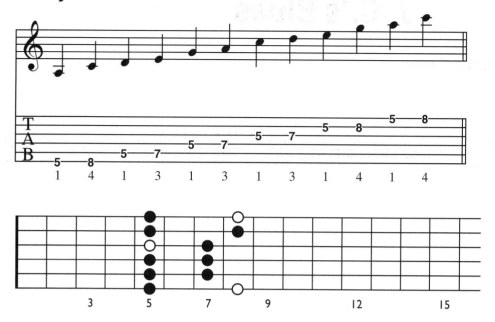

C Blues Scale

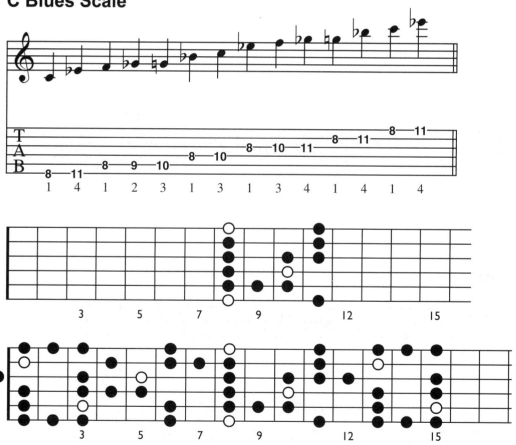

Form
13 choruses, you solo throughout.

Mr. Slow's Blues

Try this slow blues in C Major.

C

12/8 Medium blues in C

C Minor Pentatonic

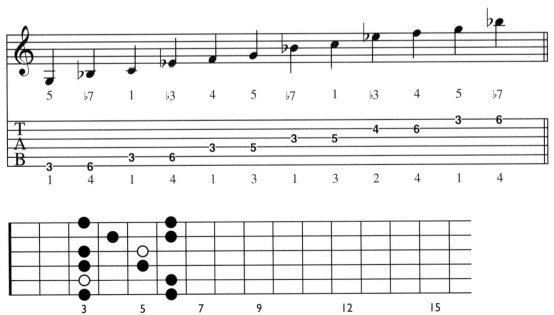

C Major Pentatonic

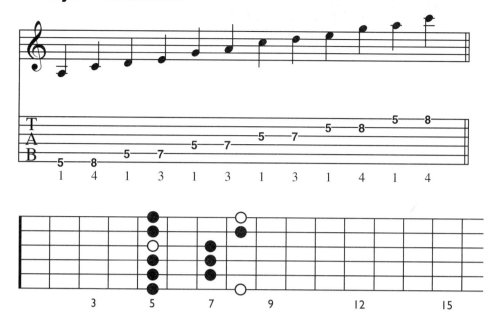

C Blues Scale

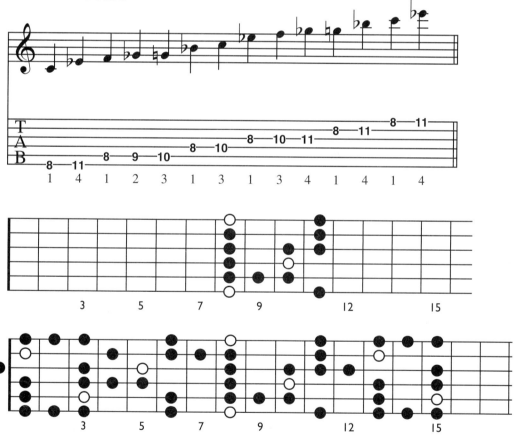

Form
6 choruses. Play rhythm on chorus 1. You solo over all other choruses.

Track 13

Bob's Bounce

This tune is a common jazz blues progression using alternate chords. It is based on the swing and bop tunes of the 1940s. You will still be playing over a I–IV–V pattern, however, additional alternate chords have been added in between. If you occasionally interject these chord changes through a couple of choruses, it will add harmonic variety to the basic I–IV–V structure. The C Blues scale will work nicely over the whole progression. In addition, refer to Appendix B for specific licks to play.

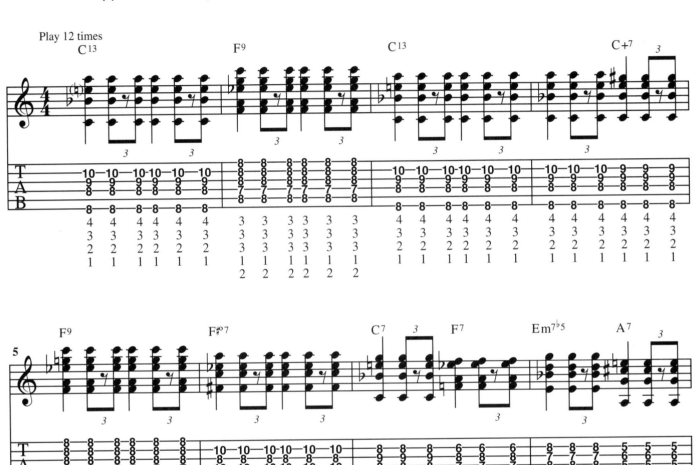

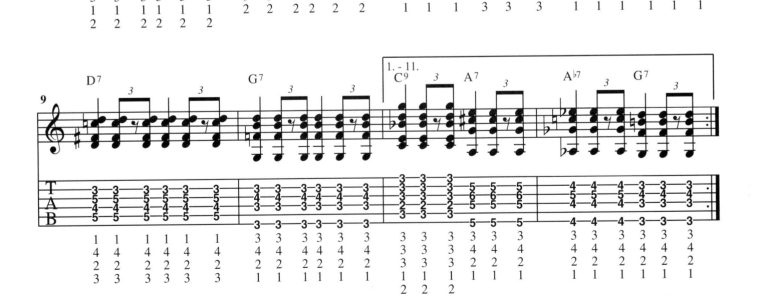

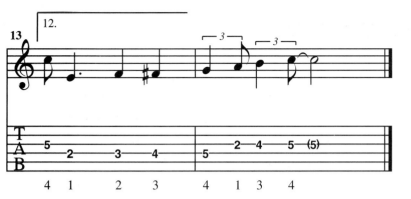

C

C Blues

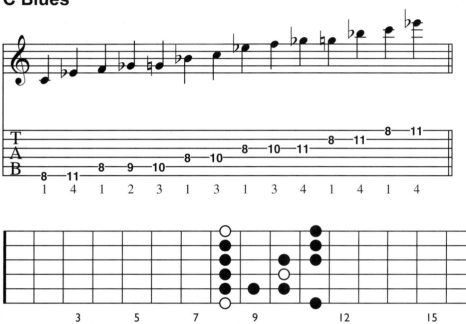

C Major Pentatonic

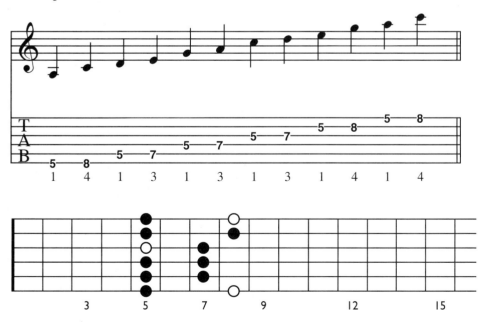

Form
Play rhythm on choruses 1, 6, 7, and 12. Solo on all other choruses.

Slow Motion

Here is a basic slow blues groove which is heard in countless songs. Keep your solos simple and soulful. Use lots of space in between your phrases and a lot of bends. The minor and major pentatonics are both equally effective here. Some great slow blues masters to listen to are Mike Bloomfield, B.B. King, Stevie Ray Vaughan, Albert King, and Otis Rush.

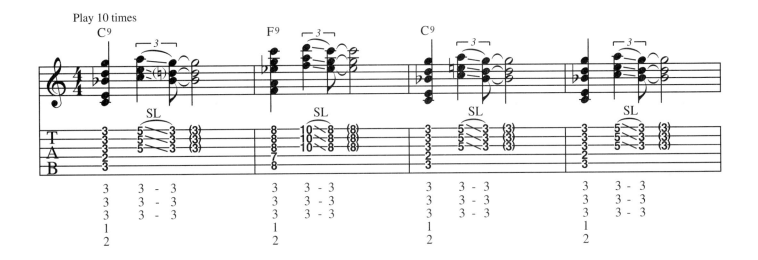

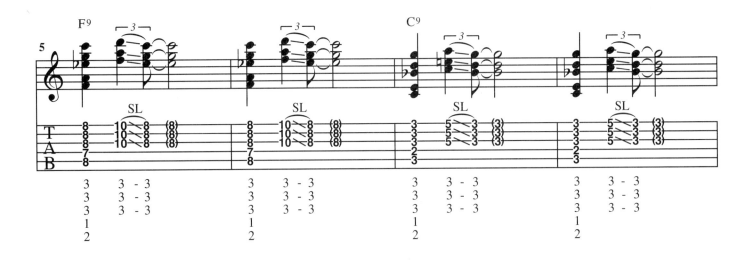

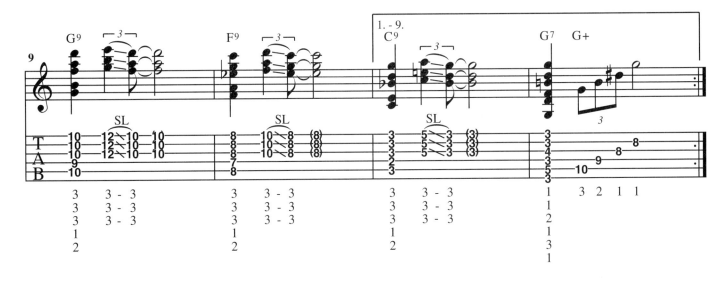

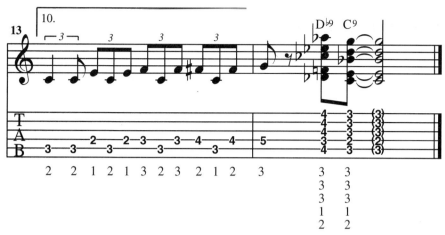

C Blues

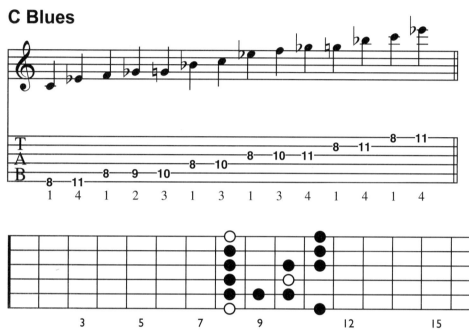

C Major Pentatonic

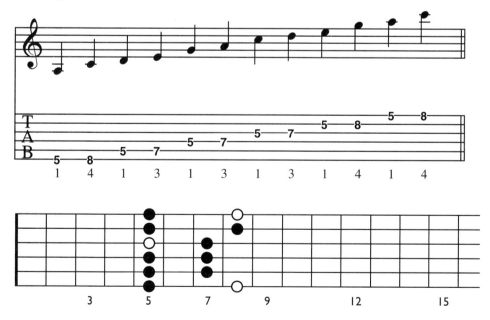

Form
Play rhythm on choruses 1, 5, 6, and 10. Solo on all other choruses.

"C" Rock

This is a standard rock blues without a *turnaround* (a musical refrain which leads back to the beginning) at the end. Use F Mixolydian on the IV7 and V7 chords instead of C Minor Pentatonic. Emphasize the 3rds (guide tones). The B section, or bridge, of the tune allows you to concentrate on playing over the IV to I progression. This is a good way to extend a blues progression. Using G Mixolydian, concentrate on the guide tones. Take your time and work on small, specific goals.

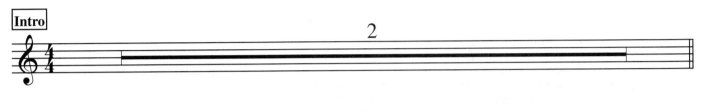

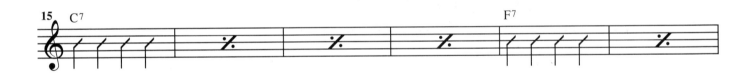

C Minor Pentatonic

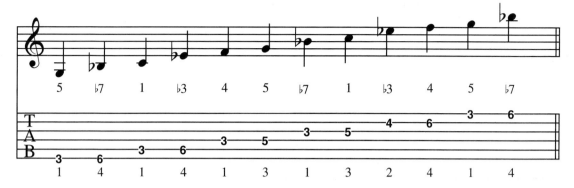

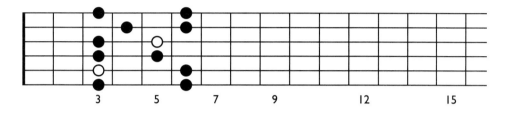

C

F Mixolydian

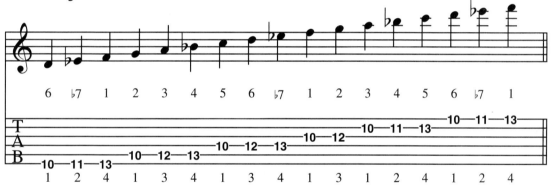

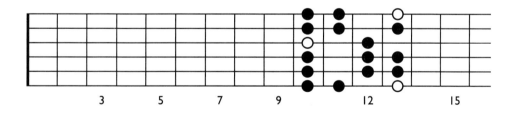

Form
Repeat entire form five times.

The Turnaround

C

This tune explores a few ways to use turnarounds. Located at the end of a progression, turnarounds can be used very effectively to top off a solo. The bass motion of the first turnaround is a common progression: I–VI–II–V (meaures 9–12). The second example has a more jazzy sound: I–♭III–♭VI–♭II (meaures 25—28). Both progressions use dominant 7th chords exclusively, so try using the Mixolydian sound. The second turnaround is a bit tricky, so start by creating a guide-tone line in half notes over the changes. Note the example below.

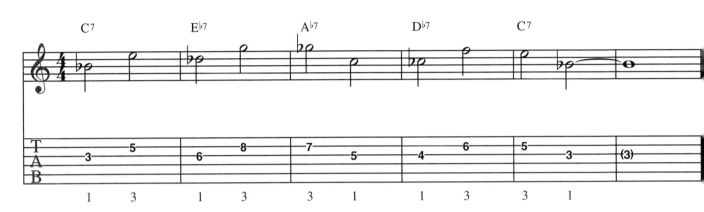

C Minor Pentatonic

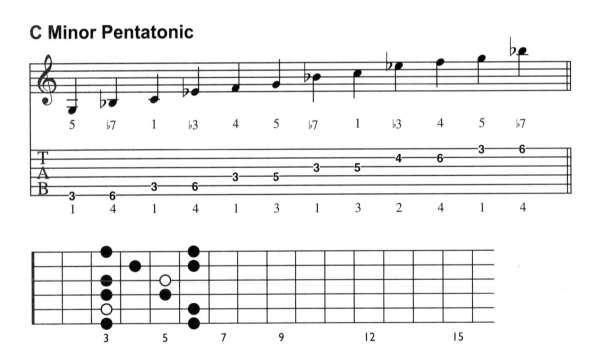

Form
Repeat the entire form 12 times.

Jazz Minor Blues

This C minor blues uses extended chords in measures 9 and 10, and also uses an augmented 7th chord in measure 12.

C

Blues in C minor

C Minor Pentatonic

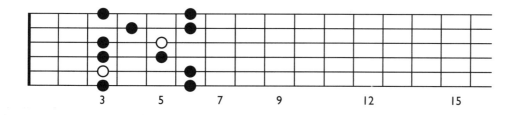

C Blues Scale

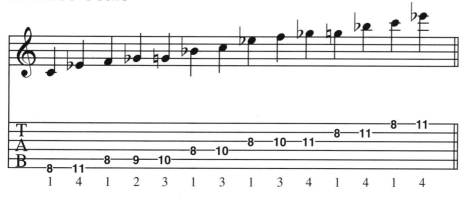

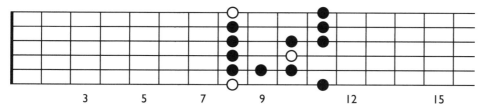

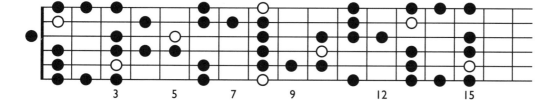

Form

10 choruses. Play rhythm on chorus 6. Last chorus has a long ending and repeats ii–V–i.

Hip Hop

This hip-hop style tune consists primarily of dominant 7th chords. In the A section, notice that these chords are not necessarily diatonically related (they do not belong together in the same key). You can play over each chord individually using the Mixolydian mode based on the root of the chord (for more scales and modes, look for *The Guitar Mode Encyclopedia*). A lot of players superimpose the Dorian mode a 5th above the root of the chord (for example, use A♭ Dorian over a D♭7 chord). Both modes sound exactly the same as they use the same pitches, however, thinking in Dorian rather than Mixolydian emphasizes a different sound, perhaps more of a jazz sound. Think simply at first and use pitches that help make the chord changes stand out. This not-so-standard blues is a gas to play over.

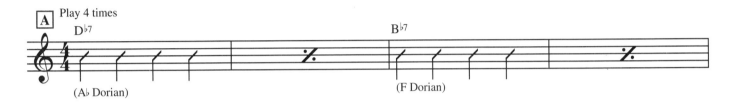

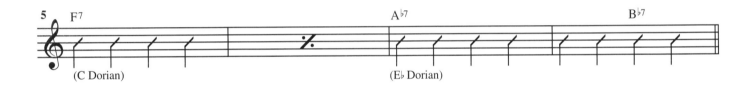

A♭ Dorian

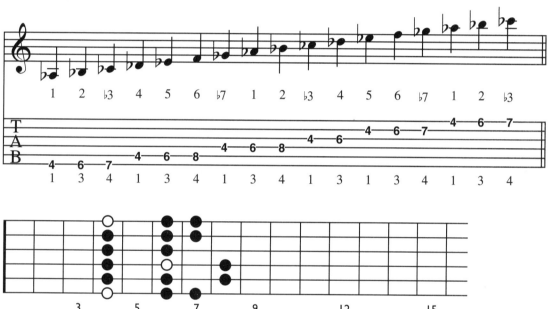

Form
Repeat entire form four times.

Let Me Go

You may recognize the main theme of this tune as being like the classic horn section riff in Otis Redding's "Can't Turn You Loose." This lick, when played by a rhythm guitar, can really drive a tune. Try an equal mix of major and minor pentatonics, using short lick patterns with some repetitive rhythmic figures.

D

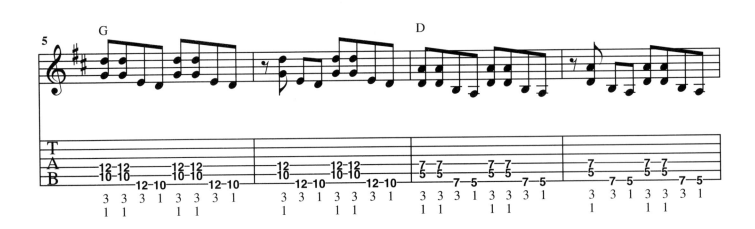

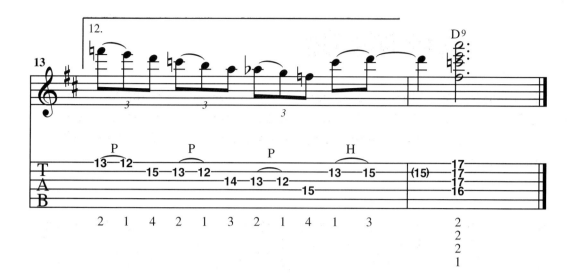

D

D Major Pentatonic

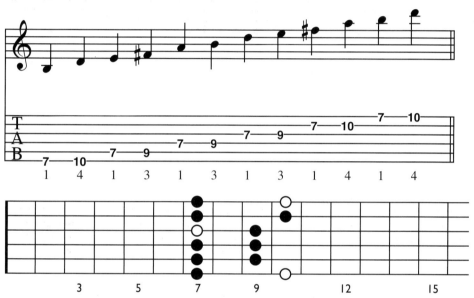

D Minor Pentatonic

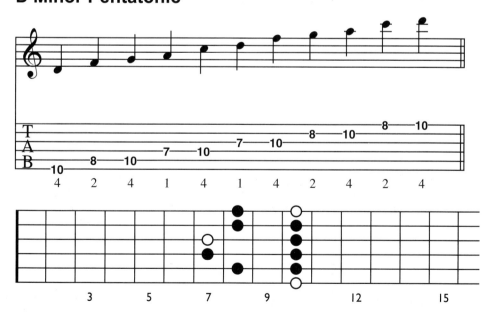

Form
Play rhythm on choruses 1, 6, 7, and 12. Solo on all other choruses.

Blue Clave

Here is a variation on a 16-bar blues with a Latin twist. Again, the chords need to be handled individually. Start simply (melodically and rhythmically). Gradually introduce longer phrases with some space between them. Straight eighths would work well over this groove. Use the symmetrical diminished scale over the G♯dim7. Notice how the scale alternates between whole steps and half steps. It may take a while to get this sound together but keep trying. It will sound great.

D

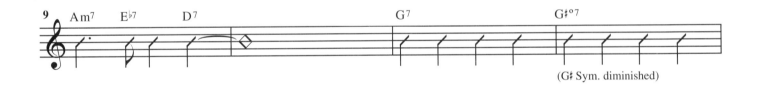

(G♯ Sym. diminished)

G♯ Symmetrical Diminished

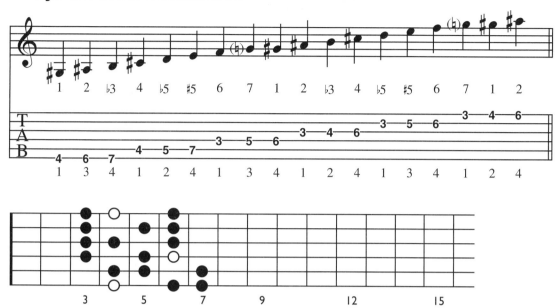

D

Form
Repeat entire song 12 times.

Track 21

Revolving Resolutions

This tune explores a fun way to apply the altered dominant scale. The [A] section moves between two dominant 7th chords a whole step away from each other. This progression is diatonic from within the melodic minor scale (between IV and V). The altered dominant scale is a perfect choice because both chords, the IV7 and V7 chords (A♭7 and B♭7), are diatonic to the key (E♭ Melodic Minor). Use the 7th mode of that scale: D Altered Dominant. Examine the relationship between the notes of this scale and each dominant 7th chord. The chords in [C] move twice as fast as in [B]. This may be complicated at first, so take your time. Play fewer notes to allow yourself time to anticipate the movement.

E♭

D Altered Dominant

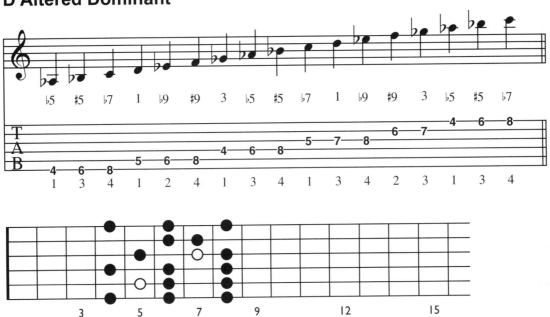

G♭ Lydian ♭7

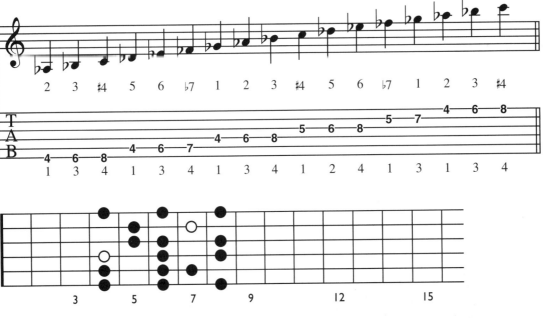

E Altered Dominant

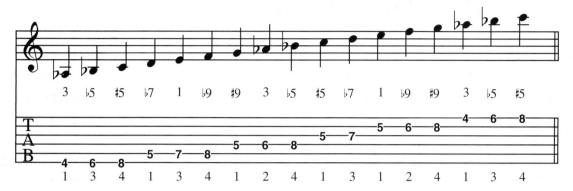

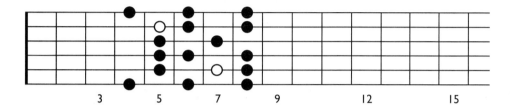

Eb

Db Major

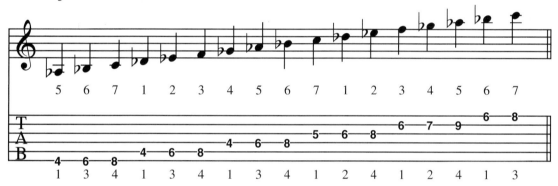

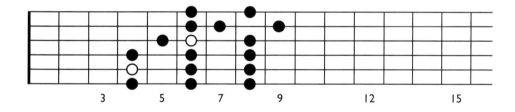

A Minor Pentatonic

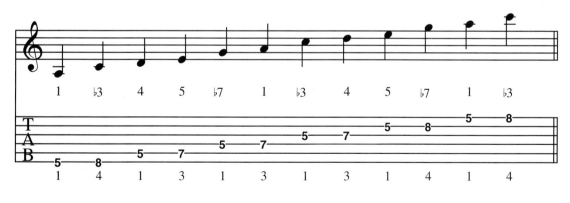

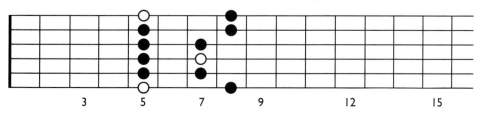

E♭

Form
Repeat entire form five times.

Joe Pass *(1929–1994)*
had a profound influence
on future guitarists. He
was fascinated by the
blues elements of jazz.

George Benson *(born*
March 22, 1943) is a
multi-Grammy Award
winning jazz guitarist
with a unique approach
to the blues. He is also
known as a pop, R&B,
and scat singer.

Track 22

J. J.'s Pink Blues

This is a standard blues in E, but watch out for the ♯9 in measure 9.

E

E Minor Pentatonic

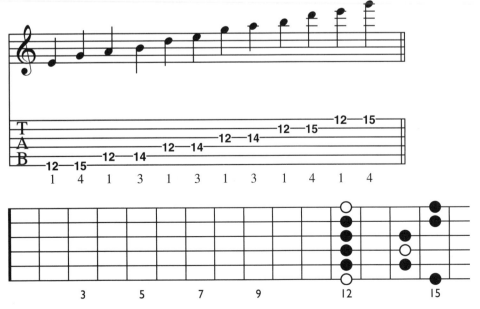

E Major Pentatonic

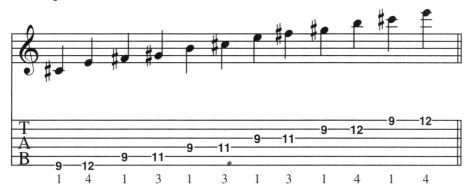

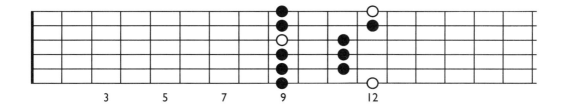

E Blues Scale

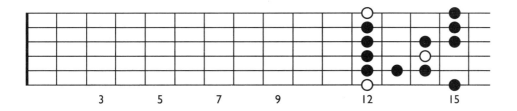

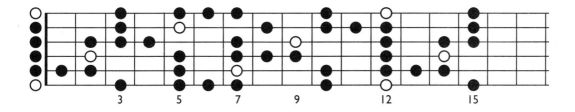

Form
9 choruses. Pattern played by 2nd guitar in choruses 1 and 2, you can solo
if you like. Choruses 3–9, you solo. Choruses 3 and 8 are in swing feel.
Long ending on last chorus.

Track 23

Shoot It Down

This funk-blues groove is in the style of Junior Walker's "Shotgun." When soloing, keep your licks simple and funky. You should mainly use the E Blues scale for this tune, although the E Dorian scale will add melodic color to your improvising.

E

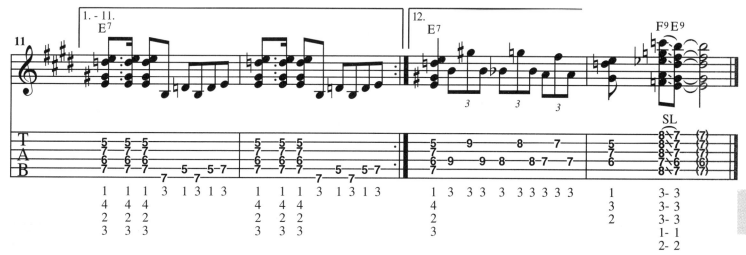

E Blues

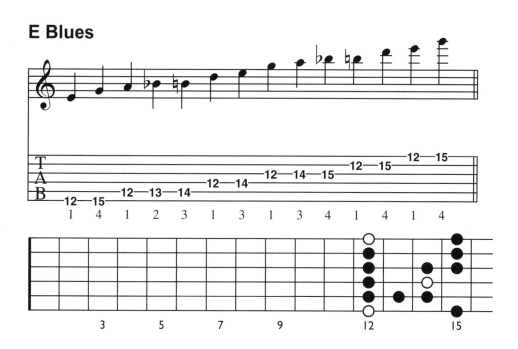

E Dorian

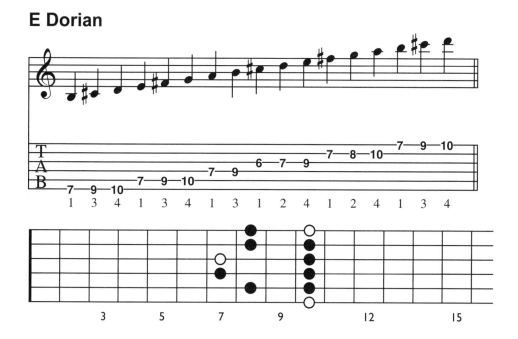

Form
Play rhythm on choruses 1, 6, 7, and 12. Solo on all other choruses.

Hand on the Range

Although this tune is still a common blues form, it is a bit more involved harmonically. The idea is to anticipate the chord changes and emphasize the guide tones. Begin by playing your solo in half notes only, then try a quarter-note solo, etc. By limiting your rhythmic ideas, you will be able to hear more melodically. You might try playing a simple guide-tone line over the progression first. This will help you hear the changes and form a harmonic skeleton on which to base your ideas. Use A Major Pentatonic over the A chord and A Natural Minor over the A Minor chord. On the next page is an example of a guide-tone line over the A section.

A Major Pentatonic

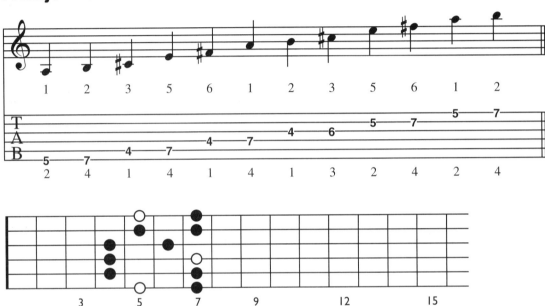

A Natural Minor

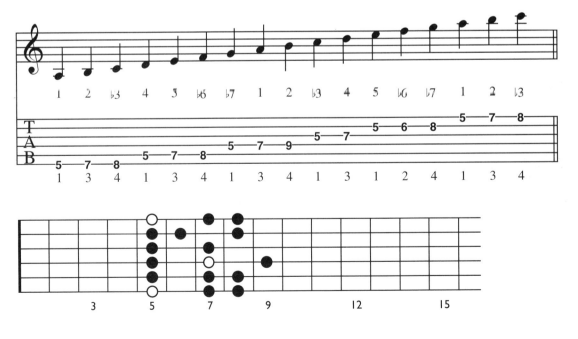

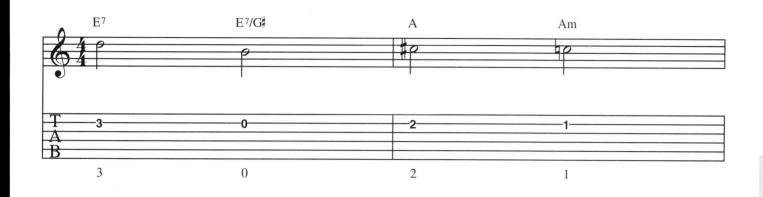

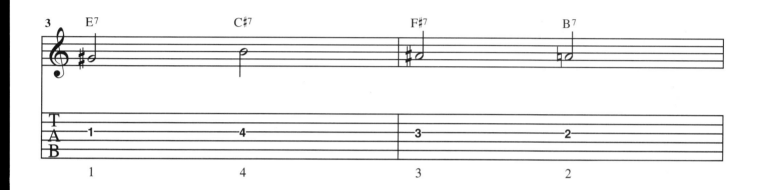

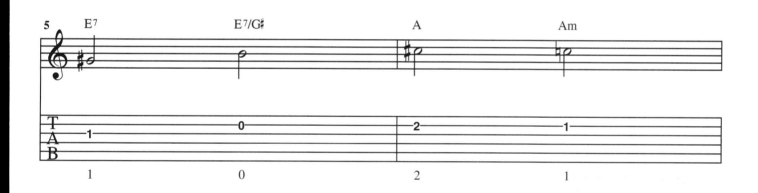

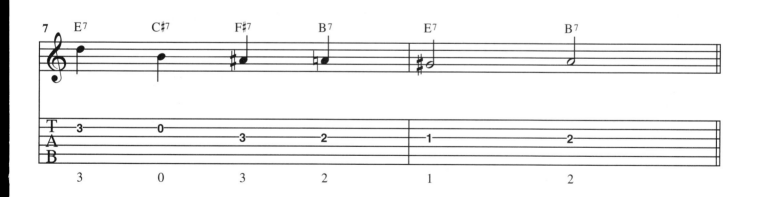

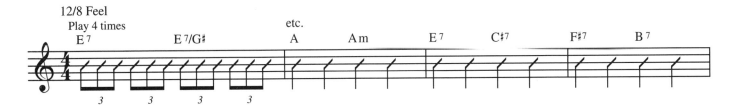

Form
Repeat entire form five times.

E

PHOTO BY KEN SETTLE

Eric Clapton *was born in Surrey, England on March 30th, 1945. He has had tremendous success in the blues and rock world. His career spans work with such bands as Derek and the Dominos (Layla) and Cream (White Room). He had solo hits such as "Wonderful Tonight" and "Tears in Heaven," but he is essentially a blues guitarist with deep roots in the genre.*

Track 25

Green's Onion Blues

This minor blues is in the style of Booker T. & the M.G.'s song "Green Onions."

E

Medium tempo blues in E minor

E Minor Pentatonic

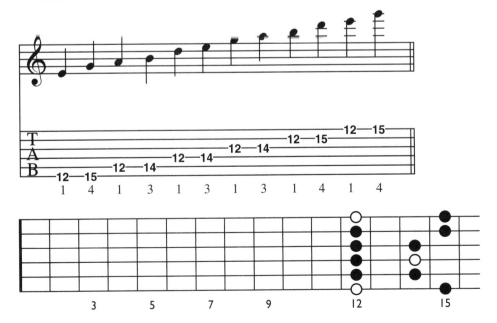

E Blues Scale

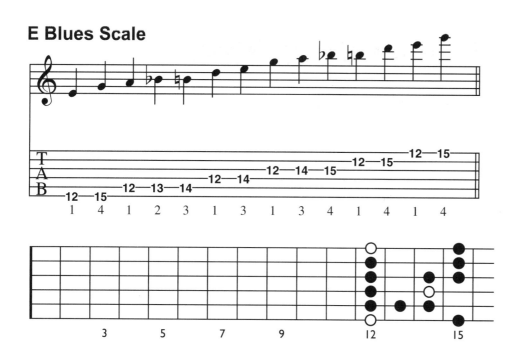

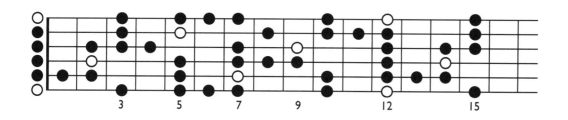

Form
12 choruses. Play rhythm on chorus 5. Long ending on last chorus.

E

Rocky's Blues

This standard minor blues progression uses slash chords in measures 10 and 12. The letter to the right of the slash is the bass note of the chord (which isn't the root).

Medium up-tempo blues in E Minor

E Minor Pentatonic

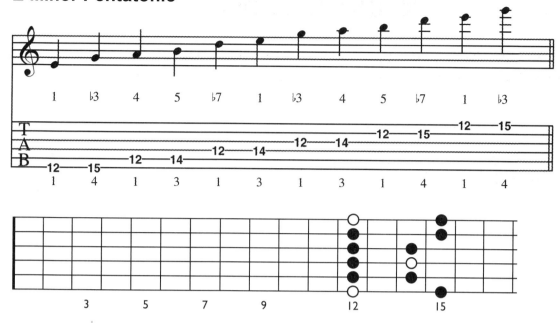

E Blues Scale

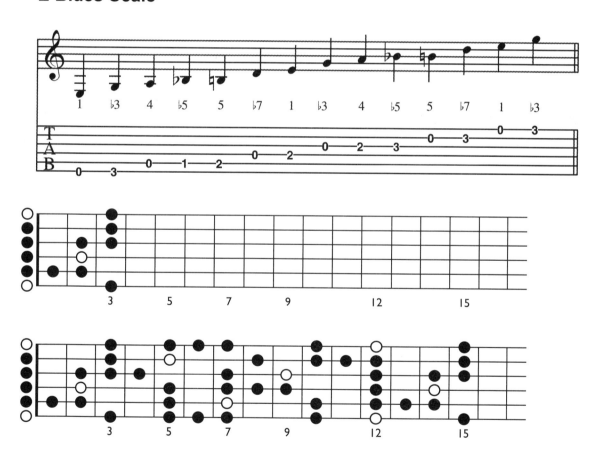

Form
12 choruses. Play rhythm on chorus 6. In the last chorus, the first chord is played over and over.

Dark Blue

This tune includes a typical minor blues pattern found in at least one cut of any blues album. Robert Cray is a good player to listen to for minor blues material. The E Blues scale works perfectly over the I chord (Em7) because the notes of an Em7 chord are all present in the scale. The E Minor scale (which is also known as E Natural Minor or E Aeolian Mode) is particularly effective over the IV chord (Am7) and the V chord (Bm7).

E

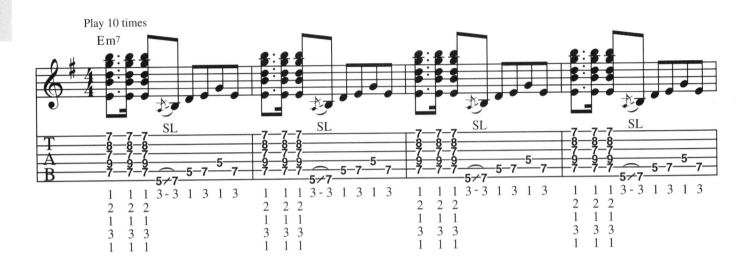

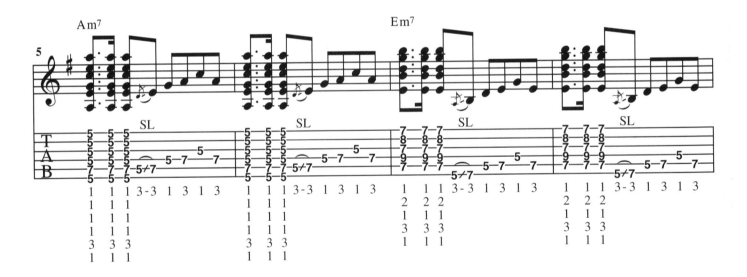

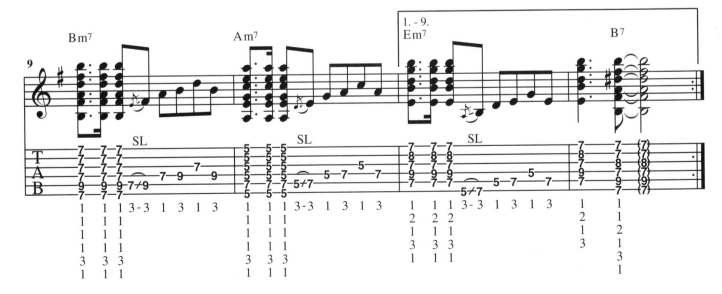

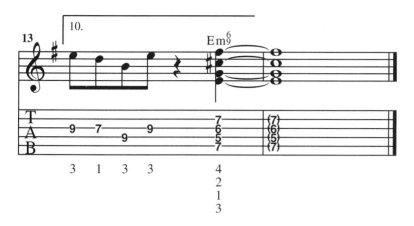

E Blues

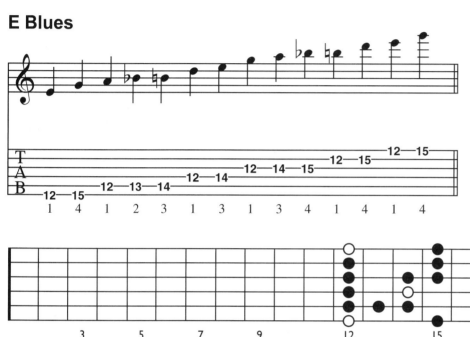

E Natural Minor

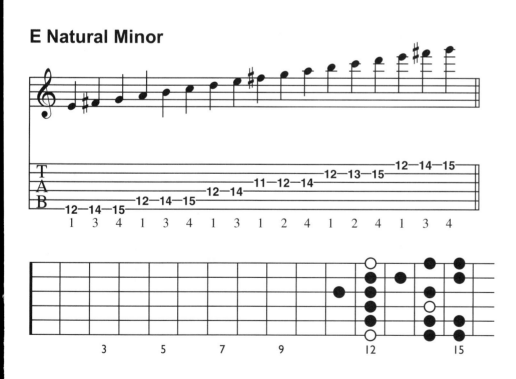

Form

Play rhythm on choruses 1, 5, 6, and 10. Solo on all other choruses.

Mr. Slow's #2

This is a standard blues in G.

12/8 Slow blues in G

G

G Minor Pentatonic

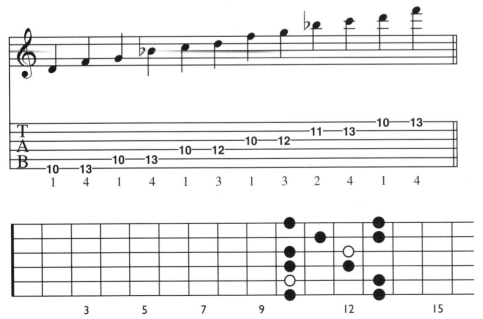

G Major Pentatonic

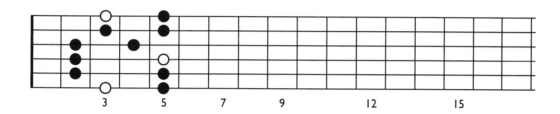

G Blues Scale

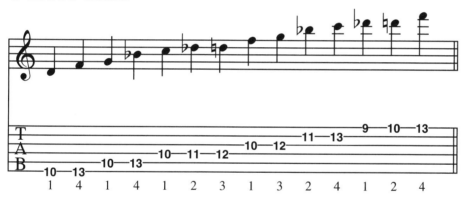

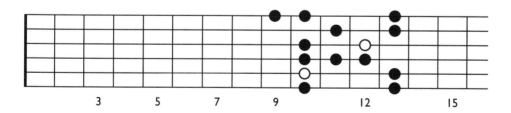

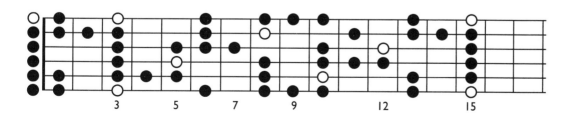

G

Form
7 choruses. Play rhythm on chorus 4. Solo for the rest.

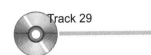

B. S. Shuffle Blues

Before you play this one, listen to the recording so you can lock into the shuffle groove.

Shuffle blues in G with horns!

G

G Minor Pentatonic

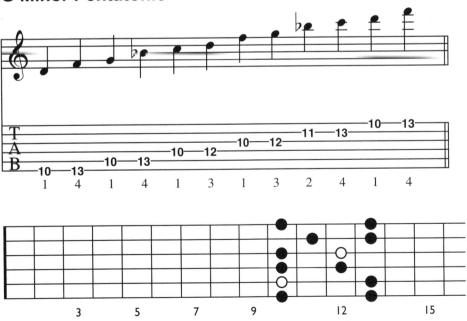

G Major Pentatonic

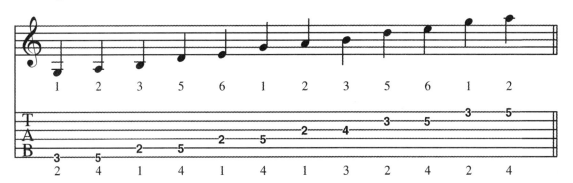

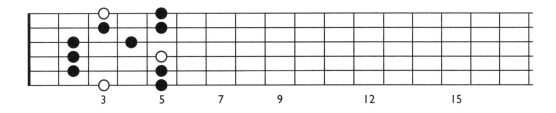

G Blues Scale

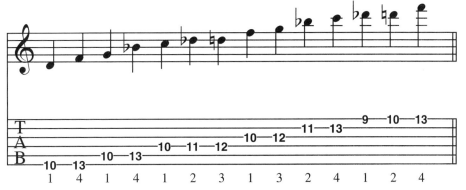

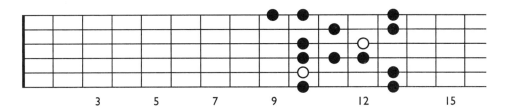

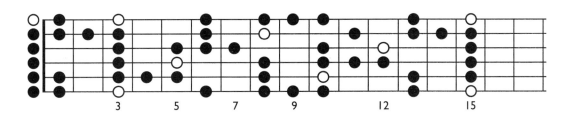

Form

8 choruses. You can play rhythm or solo over chorus 1. The horns play background parts in choruses 4, 7, and 8. Play rhythm on chorus 6 while the horns solo.

G

Track 30

Sweet Groove

This tune uses a standard blues riff that can be played by the guitar and bass together instead of a chordal pattern. Players like Eric Clapton, Buddy Guy, and Freddie King have been known to use this kind of groove. The minor pentatonic scale works well over the whole chart, but try G Dorian occasionally for a melodic rock effect.

Play 12 times

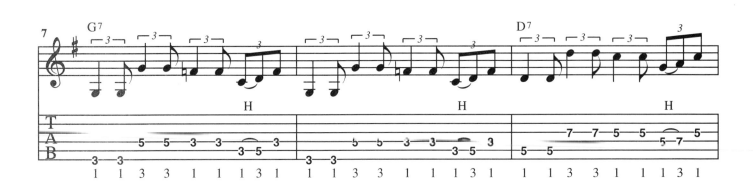

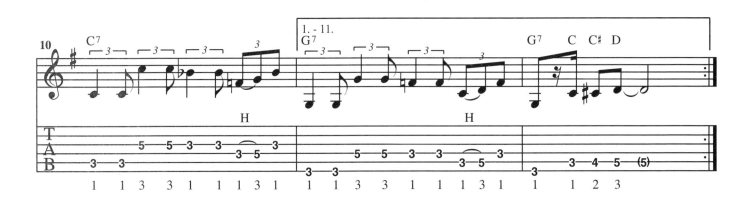

G Minor Pentatonic

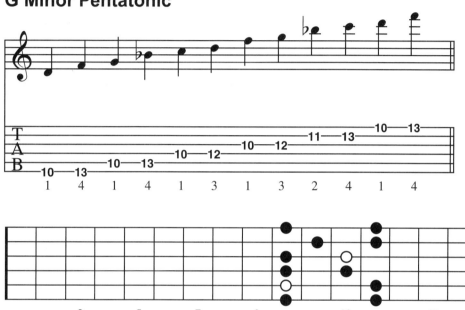

G Dorian

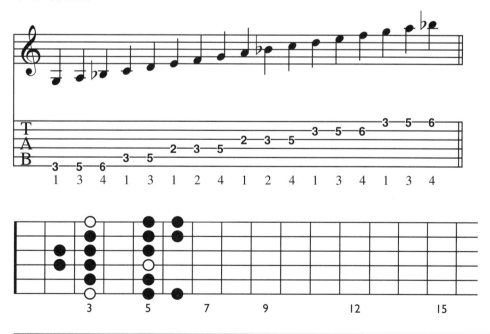

Form

Play rhythm on choruses 1, 6, 7, and 12. Solo on all other choruses.

Open Road

This eight-bar blues format is based on Big Bill Broonzy's "Key to the Highway." The chords move quickly, so stay alert and pay attention to where you are when you solo. The V chord (D) in the second measure gives this blues progression its unique character. Many gospel tunes use this progression. When you are soloing, use notes that are in the scales below, especially over the C and D chords. Refer to Appendix B on page 77 for lick ideas.

G

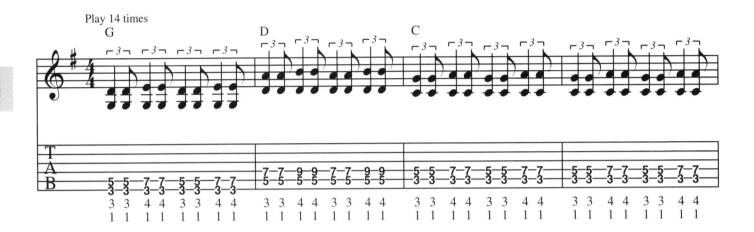

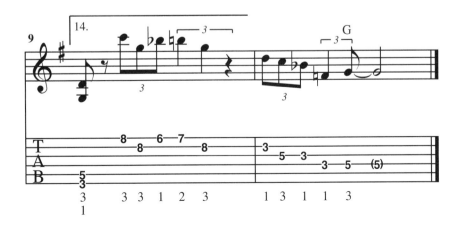

G Blues

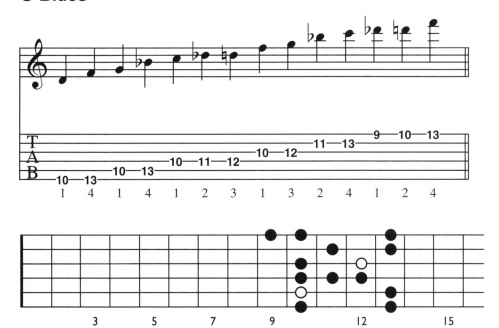

E Blues

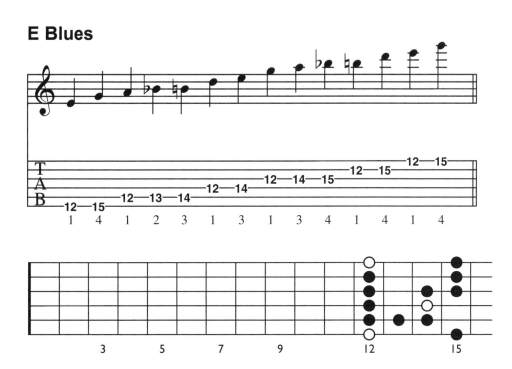

Form
Play rhythm on choruses 1, 7, 8, and 14. Solo on all other choruses.

G

Sayin' More Over I to IV

The movement of the first two chords of a blues progression, I7 to IV7, requires a lot of attention. Instead of just playing the minor pentatonic "blues scale," think of the chords individually and use the Mixolydian mode for each one. Learn the relationship between the pitches in the scale and how each one relates to the chord. When playing over the changes, use the guide tones (pitches which define the quality of the chord—3rds, 7ths, altered 5ths) to create a guide-tone line. For example, when moving from G7 to C7, the pitch B (the 3rd of G7) can move a half step down to B♭ (the 7th of C7). This kind of approach will help you create a more personal, melodic line.

G

G Mixolydian

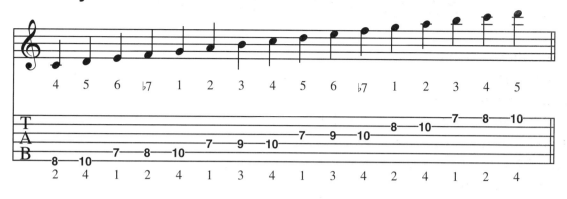

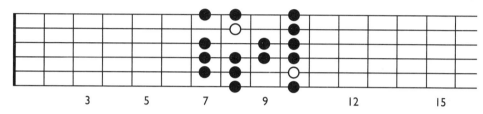

C Mixolydian

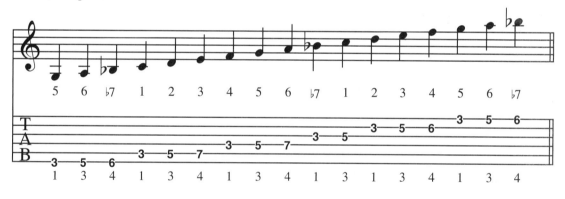

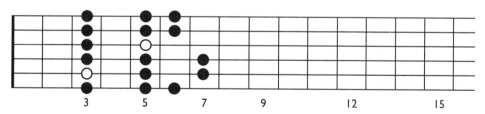

G

Form
Repeat entire form six times.

Track 33

Country Fingerstyle Blues

This tune gives you a chance to relax. It is a simple fingerstyle blues in A♭ with a cool turnaround. Again, try to treat each chord individually and experiment with guide-tone lines. Use the Mixolydian mode or, as we have been doing already (see page 38), superimpose the Dorian mode.

A♭

Form
Repeat entire song 12 times.

A♭ Mixolydian

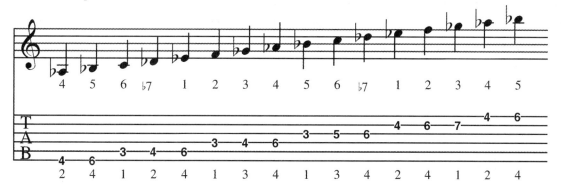

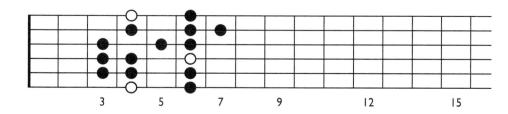

A♭ Dorian

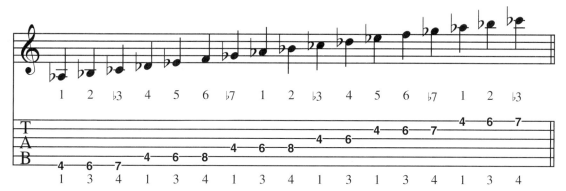

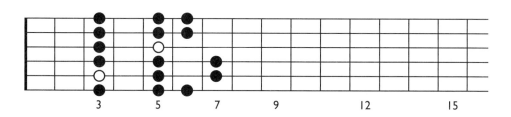

A♭

Appendix A: Tune Melodies

Page 8, Track 3, "Hide and Seek"

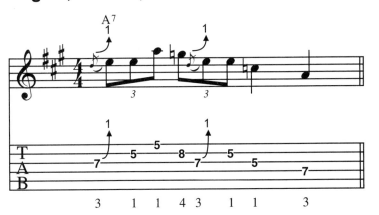
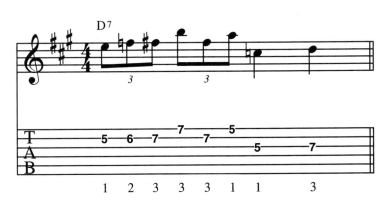

Page 10, Track 4, "Six Floors Under"

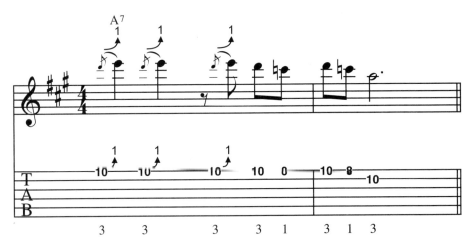

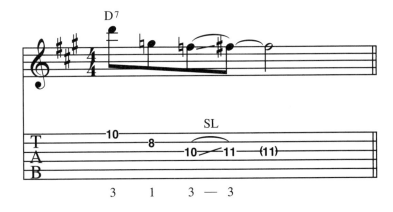

Page 18, Track 8, "Every Day with the Blues"

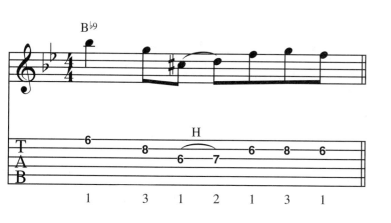
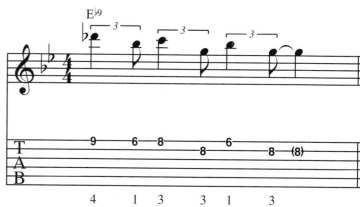

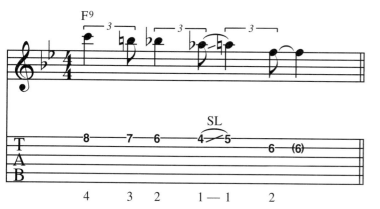

Page 30, Track 14, "Slow Motion"

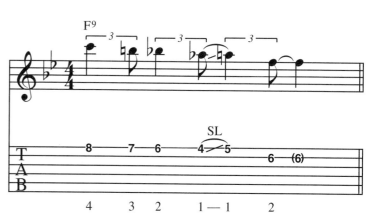

Page 60, Track 27, "Dark Blue"

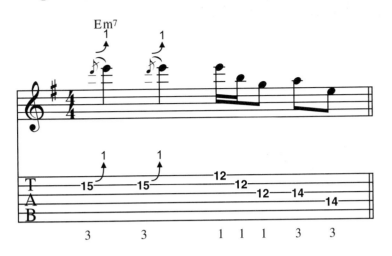

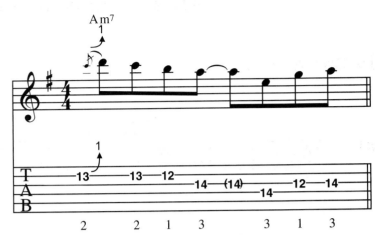

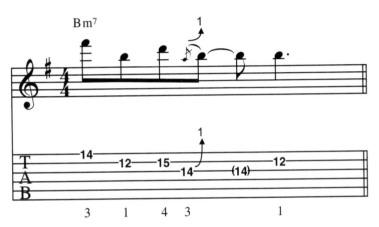

Page 68, Track 31, "Open Road"

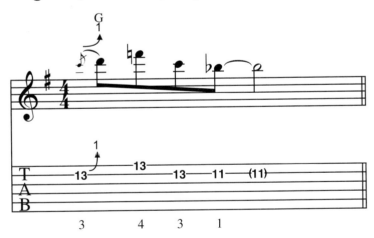

*Last time play 8va

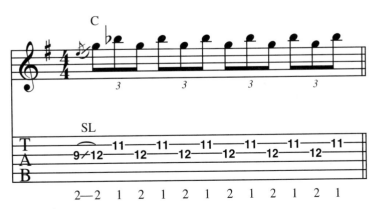

Appendix B: Assorted Licks

IV Chord Licks

#1

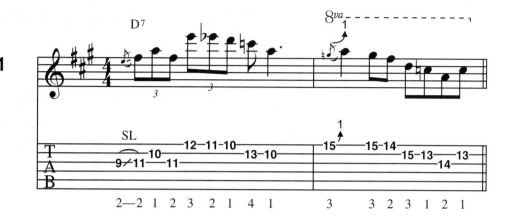

#2

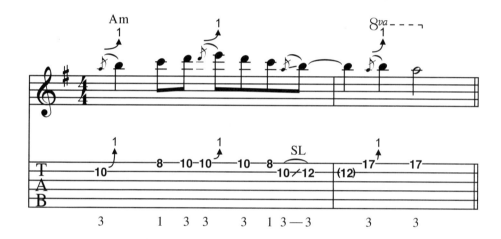

#3

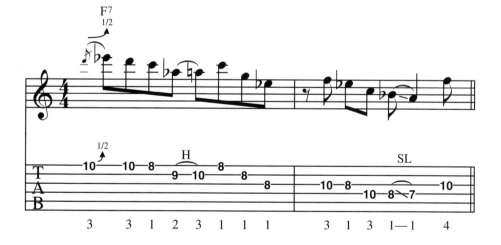

#4

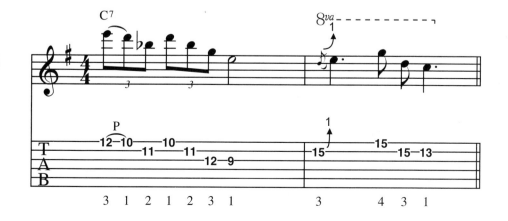

#5

#6

V Chord Licks

#1

#2

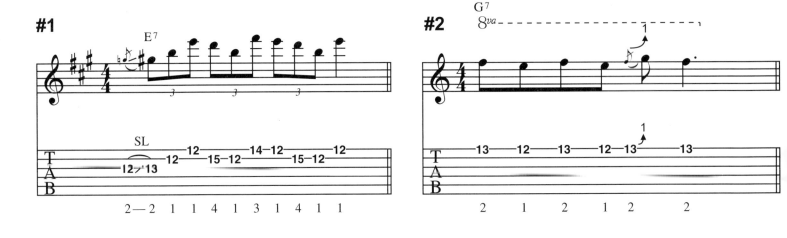

#3

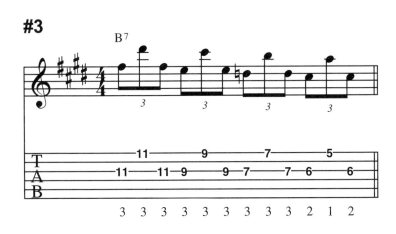

Notes

Guitar Fingerboard Chart
Frets 1–12

STRINGS

6th	5th	4th	3rd	2nd	1st
E	A	D	G	B	E

FRETS

STRINGS

Fret	6th	5th	4th	3rd	2nd	1st
Open	E	A	D	G	B	E
1st Fret	F	A#/B♭	D#/E♭	G#/A♭	C	F
2nd Fret	F#/G♭	B	E	A	C#/D♭	F#/G♭
3rd Fret	G	C	F	A#/B♭	D	G
4th Fret	G#/A♭	C#/D♭	F#/G♭	B	D#/E♭	G#/A♭
5th Fret	A	D	G	C	E	A
6th Fret	A#/B♭	D#/E♭	G#/A♭	C#/D♭	F	A#/B♭
7th Fret	B	E	A	D	F#/G♭	B
8th Fret	C	F	A#/B♭	D#/E♭	G	C
9th Fret	C#/D♭	F#/G♭	B	E	G#/A♭	C#/D♭
10th Fret	D	G	C	F	A	D
11th Fret	D#/E♭	G#/A♭	C#/D♭	F#/G♭	A#/B♭	D#/E♭
12th Fret	E	A	D	G	B	E

Fingerboard note positions (6th 5th 4th 3rd 2nd 1st strings):

- 1st Fret: F, A#/B♭, D#/E♭, G#/A♭, C, F
- 2nd Fret: F#/G♭, B, E, A, C#/D♭, F#/G♭
- 3rd Fret: G, C, F, A#, D, G
- 4th Fret: G#/A♭, C#/D♭, F#/G♭, B, D#/E♭, G#/A♭
- 5th Fret: A, D, G, C, E, A
- 6th Fret: A#/B♭, D#/E♭, G#/A♭, C#/D♭, F, A#/B♭
- 7th Fret: B, E, A, D, F#/G♭, B
- 8th Fret: C, F, A#/B♭, D#/E♭, G, C
- 9th Fret: C#/D♭, F#/G♭, B, E, G#/A♭, C#/D♭
- 10th Fret: D, G, C, F, A, D
- 11th Fret: D#/E♭, G#/A♭, C#/D♭, F#/G♭, A#/B♭, D#/E♭
- 12th Fret: E, A, D, G, B, E